HUMAN NATURE
Spirit, Mind and Flesh

Dirk Waren

Soaring Eagle Press

HUMAN NATURE: Spirit, Mind and Flesh

Unless otherwise indicated, all Scripture quotations are taken from the Holy Bible, New International Version®. NIV®. Copyright © 1973, 1978, 1984, 2011 by the International Bible Society. Used by permission of Zondervan Bible Publishers.

Other translations are listed in the **Bibliography**.

All underlining, italics and bracketed notes in scriptural quotes are added by the author.

Pronominal references to Deity in this work are not usually capitalized.

Edited by KEEII with special thanks to Raquel J. for assistance.

ISBN: 979-8-218-65907-3
PUBLISHED BY SOARING EAGLE PRESS
Youngstown

Printed in the United States of America

And the LORD God formed man of the dust of the ground, and breathed into his nostrils the breath of life; and man became a living soul.

- Genesis 2:7

CONTENTS

6

<u>1</u>

Introduction to HUMAN NATURE

Understanding human nature is important because it helps you comprehend yourself, as well as other people. It helps you to fathom or discern behaviors, motives and bondages. The Bible says that knowledge is power (Proverbs 24:5) and the Lord said it's the truth that sets people free (John 8:31-32). The Greek word for 'truth' is *alétheia (ah-LAY-thee-ah)*, which means "the way it really is." In other words, truth is **reality**.

As such, properly understanding the *reality* of human nature will naturally help you walk in victory over the dark side of your psyche and mental/spiritual illnesses. You can then, in turn, help others with the same knowledge and freedom you've acquired.

There has been much debate in the Church on the subject of human nature. Some teach that people are essentially a dichotomy (two-part) consisting of the inner person—soul/spirit—and an outer person—body. Others maintain that we are a trichotomy (three-part) consisting of two separate inner facets—spirit and soul/mind—and an outer facet—body. Others point out that human beings are essentially one psychosomatic unit by nature and therefore terms that the Bible uses, like "soul," "spirit," "mind," "body" and "heart," are ways of looking at the individual from different angles.

One popular description of human nature that I hear often is "man is a spirit that possesses a soul and lives in a body." Although this description isn't entirely biblically accurate, it's workable to some degree as long as you understand that "soul" in this context refers to the mind.

Our goal in this study is to examine all the relevant passages that apply to human nature and discern how they fit together. In the process, we'll determine the most obvious and accurate definition of the human being.

The four sound hermeneutical guidelines we'll follow are:

1. Context is king, which means that the surrounding text helps properly interpret the verse in question, including the key words thereof.
2. Scripture interprets Scripture, which means that other texts in the Bible on the same topic help interpret the one examined, with the clearer, more detailed passages trumping the more ambiguous, less detailed ones.
3. If figurative language is used, look for the glaring truth conveyed in the symbolism.
4. If the plain sense makes sense—and is line with what the rest of the Bible says on the topic—don't look for any other sense lest you end up with nonsense.

Most of the confusion over the subject of human nature can be traced to three problems:

- Lack of depth in biblical studies, such as refusing to consider relevant passages.
- A narrow view of the Hebrew and Greek words for "soul," "spirit" and so on.
- Being influenced (pressured) by one's favored minister or sect to draw a certain conclusion, which is sectarianism.[1]

The purpose of this book is to see what the Bible has always clearly taught on the subject and avoid these three interpretational ruts. In doing this, the scriptural truth should be plain to see.

I should add that spellings and pronunciations of Hebrew and Greek words are based on the scholarship of Bible Hub and Strong's lexicon.

---

[1] For important details on sectarianism, see the article at the Fountain of Life (FOL) site *SECTARIANISM — What Is It? What's Wrong With It?*

<u>2</u>

Humans Were Created as "LIVING SOULS"

There's an interpretational guideline called the 'law of first mention,' which suggests that the first mention of a word or topic in Holy Scripture is vital to fully grasping a complex theological concept. With this understanding, let's begin our study with what theologians fittingly call "the creation text." This is the passage in the first book of the Bible that describes precisely how God created human beings:

> **And the LORD God formed man of the dust of the ground, and breathed into his nostrils the breath of life; and man became a living <u>soul</u>** *(nephesh).*
>
> **Genesis 2:7 (KJV)**

> **The LORD God formed the man from the dust of the ground and breathed into his nostrils the breath of life and the man became a living <u>being</u>** *(nephesh).*
>
> **Genesis 2:7**

We see here that God created the human body out of "the dust of the earth,"[2] breathed into it "the breath of life" and so the man became "a living soul" (KJV) or "living being" (NIV).

The Hebrew word for "soul" or "being" is *nephesh (neh-FESH)*. We know that *nephesh* is equivalent to the Greek *psuche (soo-KHAY)* because when this creation text is partially quoted in 2 Corinthians 15:45, *nephesh* is translated by the word *psuche* in the original text. The Greek *psuche* is incidentally where we get the English words psyche, psychology and psychiatry.

As you can see, this foundational passage plainly states that human beings are **living** **souls**. Biblically, "soul" *(nephesh/psuche)* in its **broadest sense** refers to the entire human person. I *am* a living soul; you *are* a living soul. We see this clearly in such passages as this one:

> **All the** <u>**souls**</u> *(nephesh)* **that came with Jacob into Egypt, which came out of his loins, besides Jacob's sons' wives, all the** <u>**souls**</u> *(nephesh)* **were threescore and six.**
>
> **Genesis 46:26a (KJV)**

"Souls" in this verse simply refers to the *people* who accompanied Jacob to Egypt. The New International Version translates *nephesh* in this text as "those" and "persons" respectively.

Here's another example:

---

[2] It's a scientific fact that the human body is made up of the same essential chemical elements that are in the soil. Interestingly, humanity did not discover this until recent times, but the Creator revealed it here about *3500 years ago*.

And that day Joshua took Makkedah, and smote it with the edge of the sword, and the king thereof he utterly destroyed, them, and all the <u>souls</u> *(nephesh)* that were therein; he let none remain:

Joshua 10:28a (KJV)

"Souls" here likewise refers to the *people* that Joshua and his troops slew. The NIV translates *nephesh* in this verse as "everyone."

In both of these examples, and numerous other passages, it is clear that "soul" does not refer to the immaterial facet of human beings—which is how "soul" is popularly understood—but rather to the **whole person**. However, it's understandable why the average English-speaking reader would fail to see this because, in most translations of the Bible, *nephesh* is **not** rendered as "souls" in these verses, but rather as "those," "persons," "everyone," "people" and so on.

Here are a couple examples from the New International Version where *nephesh* is translated as "people":

… and the <u>people</u> *(nephesh)* they had acquired in Haran,

Genesis 12:5b

There were 4,600 <u>people</u> *(nephesh)* in all.

Jeremiah 52:30b

And here's an example from the New Testament where *psuche*—the Greek equivalent to *nephesh*—is translated as "people":

In it [Noah's ark] **only a few <u>people</u>** *(psuche),* **eight in all, were saved…**

1 Peter 3:20b

Once again, we see that "soul" *(nephesh/psuche)* **in its broadest sense** clearly refers to *the whole person, the whole human being—spirit, mind and body*. When *nephesh/psuche* is used in this **broad sense**, "being" is perhaps the best translation. This is why the NIV translators decided to render *nephesh* as "being" in the creation text, Genesis 2:7—the first human was a "living being."

3

THE HUMAN BEING:
Sprit, Mind and Body

According to Scripture, human beings (souls) have three facets—spirit, mind and body. This will become clearer as our study progresses. All three of these key parts are somewhat interconnected and God designed them to function as a unit. The Hebrew and Greek words for "soul"—*nephesh* and *psuche*—can refer to *any* **one** of these three facets depending on the context of the passage.

For evidence of this, let's start with verses where *nephesh*—"soul"—refers specifically to the **body:**

> " 'He [the high priest] **must not enter a place where there is a dead <u>body</u>** *(nephesh).*' "
>
> **Leviticus 21:11a**

> **"Whoever touches the dead <u>body</u>** *(nephesh)* **of anyone will be unclean for seven days."**
>
> **Numbers 19:11**

The Hebrew word *nephesh* in these passages refers to the body, but not to mind or spirit. This is obvious because a dead body possesses neither mind nor spirit. There are a couple of other **such examples in the Bible.**

Nephesh or *psuche*—"soul"—can also refer specifically to the human **mind**. The mind itself possesses three vital qualities: **volition** (will), **emotion** (feeling) and **reason** (thinking). As such, the mind is the decision-making center of your being. Here are a couple examples of *nephesh/psuche* used in reference to the mind:

> **"And you, my son Solomon, acknowledge the God of your father, and serve him with wholehearted devotion and with a willing <u>mind</u> (*nephesh*), for the LORD searches every heart and understands every motive behind the thoughts.**
>
> **1 Chronicles 28:9a,b**

> **But the Jews who refused to believe stirred up the Gentiles and poisoned their <u>minds</u> (*psuche*) against the brothers.**
>
> **Acts 14:2**

The first text speaks of Solomon's "willing mind." We know that *nephesh* in this case refers to the mind because the mind is the center of volition and will. It is the mind that makes willful decisions.

The second passage speaks of the Jews who poisoned the minds of the Gentiles. We know that *psuche* in this verse refers to the mind because the Jews obviously corrupted the reasoning faculties of the Gentiles so they would make a willful decision to reject the gospel.

Nephesh/psuche—"soul"—can also refer specifically to the **human spirit,** as observed here:

> **And Mary said:**
> "My <u>soul</u> *(psuche)* **glorifies the** Lord
> [47]**and my <u>spirit</u>** *(pneuma)* **rejoices in God my**
> **savior.**"   Luke 1:46-47

This is an example of synthetic parallelism, a type of Hebraic poetry in which the second part of the passage explains or adds something to the first. In this case, Mary says that her "**soul**"—*psuche*—glorifies the Lord. Exactly what part of her *being* glorifies the Lord? The next verse specifies that it is her *spirit* that rejoices in God.

Hence, "soul"—*psuche*—a term used in its broadest sense for the whole human being, refers here *specifically* to the spirit, which is the part of a person that "delights in God's law" (Romans 7:22; Matthew 26:41). You could call it your good side—the part of you that opposes the sinful nature. (We'll look at this further next chapter).

Also, *nephesh* is translated as "spirit" five times in the Old Testament in the original New International Version.

"Soul" Used in Reference to the Entire Immaterial Being—Mind & Spirit

The Hebrew and Greek words *nephesh* and *psuche* at times refer to *both* mind and spirit—the entire immaterial being as **separate** from the body. Here's a good example:

> **And he** [Elijah] **stretched himself upon the** [dead]
> **child three times, and cried unto the LORD, and**
> **said, O LORD my God, I pray thee, let this child's**
> <u>**soul**</u> *(nephesh)* **come into him again.**
>   **1 Kings 17:21 (KJV)**

Elijah is praying that the boy's immaterial being ("soul")—his mind and spirit—return to the kid's dead body. The whole *immaterial* being of people is their invisible **life force**, their **very life**. In other words, it is the mind and spirit that gives life to a body of flesh that would otherwise be dead. This is why the New International Version translates Elijah's prayer as "O LORD my God, let this boy's life *(nephesh)* return to him."

Here are a few other examples of *nephesh/psuche* used in reference to the **entire immaterial being** as separate from the physical body:

> **Be merciful to me, O LORD, for I am in distress;**
> **my eyes grow weak with sorrow,**
> **my soul (nephesh) and body with grief.**
>> **Psalm 31:9**

> **The glory of his forest and his fruitful land**
> **the LORD will destroy, both soul (nephesh) and body,**
> **and it will be as when an invalid wastes away.**
>> **Isaiah 10:18 (NRSV)**

> **"Rather, be afraid of the One who can destroy both soul (psuche) and body in hell."**
>> **Matthew 10:28**

All three of these passages describe human nature as decidedly two separate parts: "soul and body," which means…

- **Non-physical** and **physical**.
- **Immaterial** and **material**.

In such cases, "soul" clearly refers to **the whole immaterial being, both mind and spirit**.

Perhaps the best proof that *nephesh/psuche* can refer to the entire immaterial being is found in the book of Revelation where disembodied saints are described as "**souls**" *(psuche)* in John's vision:

> **When he opened the fifth seal, I saw under the altar the <u>souls</u> *(psuche)* of those who had been slain because of the word of God and the testimony they had maintained. [10] They called out in a loud voice, "How long, Sovereign Lord, holy and true, until you judge the inhabitants of the earth and avenge our blood?"**
>
> **Revelation 6:9-10**

> **I saw thrones on which were seated those who had been given authority to judge. And I saw the <u>souls</u> *(psuche)* of those who had been beheaded because of their testimony for Jesus and because of the word of God.**
>
> **Revelation 20:4a,b**

Whether these passages are literal or symbolic isn't important to our study (I believe they're literal because that's the plain sense of the text; as it is said: If the plain sense makes sense, don't look for any other sense lest you end up with nonsense[3]). What is important is that *psuche*—"souls"—is the biblical word used to describe disembodied people. It therefore refers to their **entire immaterial being, both mind and spirit**.

---

[3] Other reasons for taking them literally are detailed in chapter <u>10</u> of *SHEOL KNOW*. Or see the article *The Believer's INTERMEDIATE STATE (Between Physical Death and Bodily Resurrection)* at the FOL site.

The fact that "soul"—*nephesh/psuche*—can refer to the mind in certain passages (and to the spirit on rare occasions) and to **both** mind & spirit in others, explains the *seeming* interchangeability of these terms in Scripture.

The Narrow View of "Soul" Must Be Rejected

In light of this data, to properly understand what the Bible teaches about human nature, the narrow view of the term "soul" *(nephesh/psuche)* must be rejected. I say this because many ministers give the impression that "soul" only refers to the mind or that it only refers to the immaterial part of human beings. We've just seen clear biblical proof that both of these views are narrow and erroneous.

To recap, "soul" *(nephesh/psuche)* in its broadest sense refers to the *entire* human being. Depending on its context, it can also refer specifically to each one of the three facets of human nature—body, mind or spirit. It can also refer to the entire immaterial being—mind and spirit. Thus, the views that *nephesh/psuche* **only** refer to the mind or **only** refer to mind & spirit are only true in certain contexts.

Consider, for example, Paul's statement here:

> **May God Himself, the God of peace, sanctify you through and through. May your whole spirit, <u>soul</u>** *(psuche)* **and body be kept blameless at the coming of our Lord Jesus Christ.**
>
> **1 Thessalonians 5:23**

Even though *psuche*—"soul"—in its broadest sense refers to the entire human person, in this context it obviously refers to the mind. We know this because spirit, mind and body are the three chief facets of human nature. Hence, *psuche* must refer to the mind in this verse. This is in line with the hermeneutical rule 'context is king.'

Or consider this passage:

> **For the word of God is living and active, sharper than any double-edged sword, it penetrates even to dividing <u>soul</u>** *(psuche)* **and spirit, joints and marrow; it judges the thoughts and attitudes of the heart.**
>
> **Hebrews 4:12**

"Soul" refers to the mind here because spirit and mind can be "divided" but spirit and the whole person cannot be divided since the whole person naturally includes the spirit. A person that lacks a spirit is no longer a whole person, are you following?

<u>4</u>

THE MIND'S WAR
Betwixt Flesh and Spirit

So, Paul described human nature as having three basic facets in 1 Thessalonians 5:23—spirit, mind and body—and he was led of the Holy Spirit to say this (2 Peter 1:21). Let's observe further support in Paul's inspired letter to the Romans:

> **For I know that nothing good dwells within me, that is, in my <u>flesh</u>. I can will what is right, but I cannot do it. [19] For I do not do the good I want, but the evil I do not want is what I do. [20] Now If I do what I do not want, it is no longer I that do it, but sin that dwells within me.**
>
> **[21]So I find it to be a law that when I want to do what is good, evil lies close at hand. [22]For I delight in the law of God in my <u>inmost self</u> [i.e. spirit], [23]but I see in my members another law at war with the law of my <u>mind</u>, making me captive to the law of sin that dwells in my members.**
>
> **Romans 7:18-23 (NRSV)**

Paul speaks of three facets of human nature in this passage. In verse 18 he mentions his "**flesh**" (or "sinful nature" in the NIV) and states that "nothing good dwells within" it.

In verse 22 he mentions his "inmost self" and says that this part of his being delights in God's law, referring to universal *moral* law (chronicled in the Torah). Paul was obviously speaking of his **spirit**.

In verse 23 he mentions his "**mind**" and the "war" that it is fighting. The precise nature of this "war" is made clearer just a few verses later (keeping in mind that Paul's original letter to the Romans had no chapter or verse divisions; these were added centuries later for convenience in scriptural study and citation):

> **For those who live according to the flesh set their <u>minds</u> on the things of the <u>flesh</u>, but those who live according to the <u>spirit</u> set their <u>minds</u> on the things of the <u>spirit</u>. [6]To set the <u>mind</u> on the <u>flesh</u> is death, but to set the <u>mind</u> on the <u>spirit</u> is life and peace.**
>
> **Romans 8:5-6 (NRSV) [4]**

These divinely inspired words reveal two truths: **1.** That there are three basic facets to human nature—flesh, mind and spirit; and **2.** that the mind is caught in a struggle between the other two opposing

---

[4] Since there is no capitalization in the biblical Greek, translators must determine if "spirit" should be capitalized, in reference to the Holy Spirit, or not capitalized, in reference to the human spirit. Many English translations capitalize "spirit" in these two verses and some do not (for example The New English Bible). Since this passage—and similar ones—are plainly referring to the *human* spirit, "spirit" should not be capitalized. This will be made clearer as our study progresses. In a way it makes no significant difference since the believer's reborn human spirit is **united with and led by the Holy Spirit** (Ephesians 3:16; Romans 8:16). All of this explains why I took the liberty of *uncapitalizing* "spirit" in this passage from the NRSV.

facets—flesh and spirit. This is the "war" Paul was talking about in verse 23 (of Romans 7, quoted above).

What exactly is the **mind**? The mind is your **center of being**. The Greek term for "mind" is *nous (noos),* meaning "The intellect, i.e. the mind (divine or human; in thought, feeling or will)" (Strong 50). This definition reveals the aforementioned three qualities of the human mind: **volition** (will), **intellect** (reason) and **emotion** (feeling):

The Human Mind

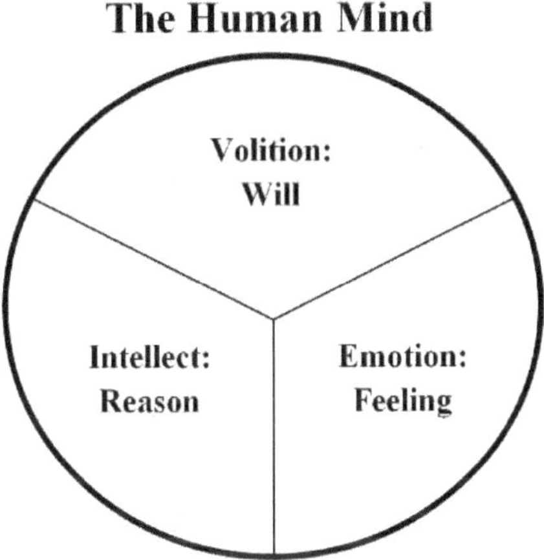

Since the mind is the center of volition and will, it is the mind that *decides* whether to live according to the flesh or according to the spirit, as the above passage points out.

What exactly are flesh and spirit? The flesh and spirit, once again, are **the conflicting facets of your being**. In Romans 7:18 above, Paul describes the flesh as the part of his being where "nothing good dwells." In verse 22 he describes his spirit as the side of him that delights in God's laws. We could therefore define flesh and spirit as follows:

- The "flesh" is the part of you that veers toward what is negative, destructive and carnal.
- Your "spirit" is the part of you that inclines toward what is positive, productive and godly.

These contrasting facets of your being are repeatedly mentioned in Scripture:

> **"Watch and pray, lest you enter into temptation. <u>The spirit</u> indeed is willing, but <u>the flesh</u> is weak."**
> **Matthew 26:41** (NKJV)

> **I say then: Walk in the spirit, and you shall not fulfill the lust of the flesh. [17]For <u>the flesh</u> lusts against <u>the spirit</u>, and <u>the spirit</u> against <u>the flesh</u>; and these are <u>contrary to one another</u>, so that you do not do the things that you wish.**
> **Galatians 5:16-17** (NKJV)[5]

As you can see, the desires of the spirit and the lusts of the flesh are in *conflict*. Since both spirit and flesh have desires, we could say that they have a voice, and each person determines which "voice" s/he will accept and follow. What do I mean by this? As noted above, your mind is the center of your being and it has the power of volition, meaning **will**. Simply put, the mind *decides*. In your mind YOU decide to live by spirit or flesh, which will in turn determine whether you are spirit-controlled or flesh-ruled. It's up to YOU.

This struggle is regularly depicted in cartoons in which a little "angel" appears near the shoulder of the protagonist contrasted by a little "devil" near the other shoulder. You'll see this in *The*

---

[5] In this quote I *un*capitalized "spirit" to match the NKJV's rendering of "spirit" in Matthew 26:41. See the previous footnote for details.

Flintstones, *The Simpsons* and, more recently, *Total DramaRama*. In other words, the conflict of flesh and spirit is universally known. Even kids grasp it!

I should point out that the desires of your spirit and your flesh are not you, but rather your *potential* you. They only become you as you DECIDE in your mind to walk according to one or the other. The way you walk according to either is by embracing and feeding the thoughts or desires of that nature. For instance, you may be in a conflict situation where your flesh flashes a crazy thought of wringing the neck of your antagonist, but does this desire make you a murderer? No. You only become a murderer if you give-in to the impulse and act on it.

It's the same thing with desires of your spirit. For instance, you might be moved to give a large sum of money to a poor family, but does this noble desire make you a generous giver? No. You only become a generous giver by embracing the impulse to grow in the grace of giving (2 Corinthians 8:7) and, then, acting on it.

Paul called the born-anew human spirit the "new self, created to be like God in true righteousness and holiness" (Ephesians 4:22-24). Your spirit is *like God* and is therefore truly righteous and holy, but does this automatically mean every believer is "like God" and truly righteous and holy, as far as practice goes? Of course not. Believers will only be "like God" (godly) and walk in true righteousness and holiness to the degree that they walk according to their spirit. Who you are in your spirit is your *potential* you; it's the way God sees you and how he wants you to be, but you'll only walk in it as **you** DECIDE to live out of your spirit and not your flesh; that is, "put on" the new self and "put off" the old self.

It's interesting to note that the formulator of psychoanalysis, Sigmund Freud, was able to discover these three basic facets of human nature through his studies. The mind is comparable to Freud's "ego"; likewise, the flesh coincides with his "id"; and the spirit corresponds to the "superego." Although I'm obviously not an advocate of Freud, pointing this out may help readers who are familiar with psychological theories to better understand the biblical model of human nature—spirit, mind and body.

I just find it fascinating that, with little or no biblical knowledge, Freud was able to discover these three key parts of human nature through simple scientific analysis. This shows that human nature is obvious to anyone who cares to honestly examine it from either an unbiased scientific or biblical approach. I am reminded of M. Scott Peck, the psychiatrist and bestselling author, who converted to Christianity not long after publishing his first book, *The Road Less Traveled*, at the age of 43. One of the main factors contributing to this decision, Peck said, was the Bible's brutally honest and accurate depiction of human nature, as illustrated here:

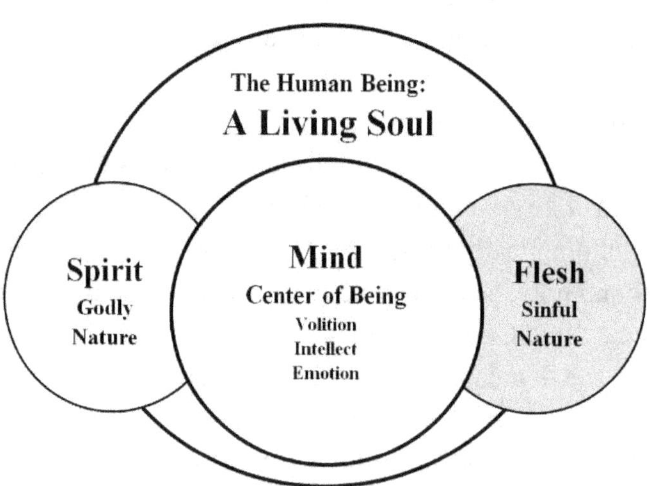

With the understanding that the human being is **a living soul consisting of spirit, mind and body**, let's take a closer look at the two opposing facets of human nature—flesh and spirit…

<u>5</u>

BODY and FLESH

The Koine Greek term for "body" is *soma* (e.g. 1 Corinthians 6:19). This word *can* also refer metaphorically to the sinful nature:

> **For we know that the old self was crucified with him so that the <u>body</u> *(soma)* of sin might be done away with, that we should no longer be slaves to sin.** **Romans 6:6**

The Greek word for "flesh" is *sarx*. Although *sarx* is most frequently used in the Bible in reference to the literal flesh of a person (e.g. John 3:6), it is often figuratively used in reference to **the sinful nature**. In such cases the New International Version understandably translates *sarx* as "sinful nature":

> **I know that nothing good lives in me, that is, in my <u>sinful nature</u> *(sarx)*. For I have the desire to do good, but I cannot carry it out.** **Romans 7:18**

30

> **The acts of the <u>sinful nature</u> _(sarx)_ are obvious: sexual immorality, impurity and debauchery; [20]idolatry and witchcraft; hatred, discord, jealousy, fits of rage, selfish ambition, dissensions, factions [21]and envy; drunkenness, orgies, and the like. I warn you, as I did before, that those who live like this will not inherit the kingdom of God.**
>
> **Galatians 5:19-21**

Both of these examples show _sarx_—"flesh"—being used as a metaphor for the carnal, sinful nature. In the first text, Paul says that "nothing good lives in" his _sarx_. He's obviously not talking about his body here. Likewise, the second passage reveals the various sinful manifestations of the _sarx_.

Because _sarx_—"flesh"—plainly refers to the **sinful nature** in such cases, I use "flesh" and "sinful nature" interchangeably throughout this book.

Soma (body) and _sarx_ (flesh) seem to be very closely related in Scripture:

> **And in him** [Christ] **you were also circumcised with a circumcision made without hands, in the removal of the <u>body</u> _(soma)_ of <u>the flesh</u> _(sarx)_ by the circumcision of Christ.**
>
> **Colossians 2:11** (NASB)

Soma (body) and _sarx_ (flesh) are so closely related in this passage that the NIV translators decided to translate them _both_ simply as "sinful nature":

In him you were also circumcised in the putting off of the <u>sinful nature</u> *(soma/sarx)*, not with a circumcision done by the hands of men but with the circumcision done by Christ.

Colossians 2:11

The conclusion we draw from the biblical data is this: Although body and flesh are not technically one and the same, it's obvious that the flesh—the sinful nature—is most closely related to the body rather than mind and spirit. In fact, the Bible tends to use body and flesh interchangeably. Because of this, I do the same in this book.

<u>6</u>

THE HUMAN SPIRIT: Your Godly Nature

Even though the flesh is most closely related to the body in Scripture, we know that it is somehow interwoven with the mind as well. We know this for certain because, if the sin nature were merely a condition of the body, then physical death would be the ultimate and absolute solution to humanity's sin problem. Needless to say, this would render Christ's death for humanity's sins pointless.

So, the flesh is somehow interwoven with the mind, which isn't helped by the unredeemed person's spirit being dead to God and lacking eternal life. Jesus thus taught that the first step in solving our sin problem is to have a spiritual rebirth. The human spirit must be regenerated. Once the spirit is reborn and becomes a "new creation," the mind needs to be "renewed" and trained so that it submits its will, intellect and emotions to the spirit and not to the flesh. This is the second step. The third and final step to solving the sin problem is to receive a new imperishable glorified body.

Before we get into all that, let's define specifically what the human spirit is and how it compels us.

The Koine Greek word for "spirit" is *pneuma (NYOO-mah)*, which corresponds to the Hebrew *ruwach (ROO-ahk)*. We've already seen in Scripture that the human spirit is that part of one's being which "delights in God's law." It's the part of your nature that inclines toward what is positive, productive and godly. In addition, it's the part of you that is aware of a spiritual dimension to reality and thus naturally attempts to 'connect' with that dimension. Only through this spiritual side of your being can you know of God and desire to connect because, as Yeshua pointed out, "God is spirit" (John 4:24). Since the flesh is one's "sinful nature," we could properly define the spirit as the "godly nature."

Both the unregenerated person and the born-again believer have a human spirit. The difference is that the non-believer is spiritually dead to God whereas the regenerated believer is spiritually alive to God. Because reborn Christians are spiritually alive to the LORD they can have a relationship, but because unredeemed people are spiritually dead to the Creator, it is *impossible* for them to have a relationship.

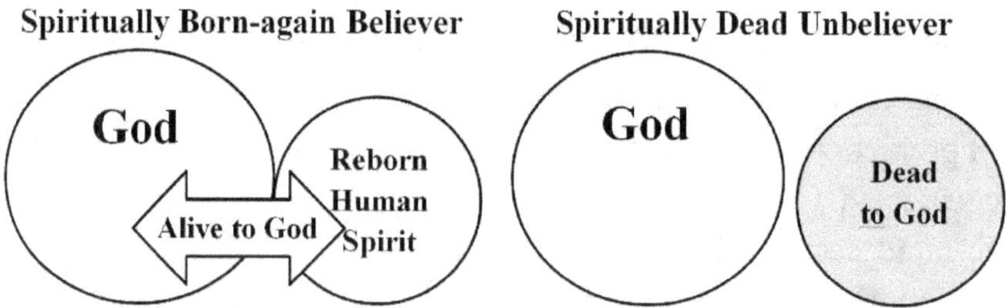

Unsaved people indeed have a spirit and therefore can be *aware* of God (or a spiritual dimension) and desire to "connect" with God (or the spiritual dimension) but they cannot connect with the Creator and have a relationship unless they are spiritually reborn. This universal attempt by humanity to connect with God (or a spiritual dimension) explains the existence of the world's numerous religions. Because we have a spiritual side to our being, human beings are—as a race—incurably religious.

The difference between religion and biblical Christianity is that **religion is humanity's attempt to connect with God**, whereas **Christianity is God connecting with humanity**. Religion is humanity's way, but biblical Christianity is God's way. Although it is certainly commendable that religious people are aware of a spiritual dimension to reality, and are attempting to connect with it—as they understand it—their attempt to unite with the Creator ultimately fails because they are spiritually dead. It is therefore, once again, not possible for them to have a relationship with God.

This is why when Yeshua's disciples asked him who could be saved, he said: "**With man this is impossible**, but not with God; all things are possible with God." (Mark 10:27). You see, salvation through the flesh—through religion—cannot be accomplished. But, with God, it's not only possible, it's available to all. That's Christianity— *real* Christianity, not the counterfeit legalism, aka Pharisaical religiosity or counterfeit 'Christianity.'

The Human Spirit Must Be "Born Again" to Connect With God

Biblical Christianity teaches that, in order to successfully unite with the Almighty and have a relationship we need to be spiritually regenerated. As Jesus plainly taught:

> **"Very truly I tell you, no one can see the kingdom of God <u>unless they are born again</u>…"**

> **⁵"Very truly I tell you, no one can enter the kingdom of God unless they are born of water and the Spirit. ⁶Flesh gives birth to flesh, <u>but the Spirit gives birth to spirit.</u>"**
>
> **John 3:3,5-6**

The Lord makes it clear in verse 3 that, in order to have a relationship with God, we must be "born again." In verse 6 he clarifies what kind of rebirth we need—*spiritual* rebirth. When a person is spiritually regenerated, the Holy Spirit gives birth to a new human spirit—the spiritual facet of his or her being is born anew! This is the "new creation" that Paul later spoke of:

> **Therefore, if anyone is in Christ, he is a <u>new creation</u>; the old has gone, the new has come.**
>
> **2 Corinthians 5:17**

"New Creation" in the Greek literally means 'a new species of being which never existed before.' The reborn spirit is "God's workmanship" (Ephesians 2:10) "created to be **like God** in true righteousness and holiness" (Ephesians 4:24). The intrinsic character of the new spirit is righteous and holy, just as God is righteous and holy. When the apostle Paul spoke of the "**treasure** in jars of clay" that he and other regenerated believers have, he was referring to the born-anew spirit, which is housed in the body or "jar of clay" (2 Corinthians 4:7).

I'm always amazed when I come across believers who either play down spiritual rebirth or deny it altogether. It's actually a **fundamental Christian doctrine**, as observed by the passages we've looked at and several others—all plain-as-day— such as Titus 3:5, 1 Peter 1:3, 1 Peter 1:23, James 1:18 and 1 John 3:9.

<u>7</u>

Your Mind Needs RENEWED

Once a person's spirit is born anew something has to be done with the mind and body, the two remaining facets of the human soul, aka human being:

> **Therefore, I urge you, brothers, in view of God's mercy, to offer your <u>bodies</u> as living sacrifices, holy and pleasing to God—this is your spiritual act of worship. [2]Do not conform any longer to the pattern of this world, but <u>be transformed by the renewing of your mind</u>. Then you will be able to test and approve what God's will is—his good, pleasing and perfect will.**
>
> **Romans 12:1-2**

> **You were taught with regard to your former way of life, to put off your <u>old self</u> [flesh], which is being corrupted by its deceitful desires; ²³<u>to be made new in the attitude of your minds;</u> ²⁴and to put on the <u>new self</u> [born-again spirit] created to be like God in true righteousness and holiness.**
>
> **Ephesians 4:22-24**

After a person is spiritually reborn, his or her body needs to be offered to God as a "living sacrifice." This means that you make a conscious decision to no longer offer the parts of your body to sin as instruments of unrighteousness, but to God's service as instruments of righteousness (Romans 6:13,19). This includes your tongue (James 4:11 & 5:9). It simply means you turn away from—repent of—behaviors that God says are unproductive or negative and start putting into practice positive and productive actions. Repentance should never be viewed as a negative thing as it means to **change your mind for the better** and, consequently, your actions.

As far as the mind is concerned, it needs to be "renewed." As you are faithful and diligent to "be made new in the attitude of your mind," you will start to be "transformed." "Transformed" is the Greek word *metamorphoo (met-ah-mor-FOH),* which means 'to change into another form.' This is obviously where we get the English word metamorphosis. Just as a worm-like caterpillar is transformed in its cocoon and emerges as a beautiful butterfly, so a wondrous metamorphosis will take place in your life as you renew your mind with the help of your guide, the Holy Spirit (John 16:13).

The second passage above shows how to successfully do this: You put off the "old self"—the flesh—by stop setting your mind on this carnal side of your being. Instead, you put on the "new self"—your reborn spirit "created to be like God in true righteousness and holiness"—by training your mind to live according to your reborn spirit:

> **Those who live according to the <u>sinful nature</u> have their <u>minds</u> set on what that nature desires; but those who live in accordance with the <u>spirit</u> have their <u>minds</u> set on what the <u>spirit</u> desires. [6]...the <u>mind</u> controlled by the <u>spirit</u> is life and peace.**
>
> **Romans 8:5-6[6]**

There's so much life, energy and peace when you train your mind to live according to your new born-anew spirit, as led of the Holy Spirit! Speaking of which, Ephesians 3:16 and Romans 8:16 show that the Holy Spirit is in union with the believer's regenerated spirit. The only reason the **Holy** Spirit can do this is because your reborn spirit was "created to be *like God* in true righteousness and **holiness**," as shown in Ephesians 4:24. Chew on that.

When the believer successfully learns to be spirit-controlled, the rebirthed spirit acts as a sort of "sixth sense," tuning you in to God and enabling you to perceive reality from the "divine viewpoint." People who are spiritually dead are limited to their five senses and consequently only perceive reality from the "human viewpoint." (Sadly, this is also true of many legitimately born-anew Christians who fail to train their minds to live according to their reborn spirit).

True and intimate knowledge of God can only be attained through this sixth sense with the help of the indwelling Holy Spirit (John 16:7,13). With this understanding, it becomes increasingly clear

---

[6] I took the liberty of *un*capitalizing "spirit" in this passage from the NIV since it's obviously contrasting the two sides of human nature, flesh and spirit. The Lord Himself did so in Matthew 26:41 & Mark 14:38. This was explained in detail in chapter <u>4</u> in the footnote regarding the same passage, Romans 8:5-6.

why the Lord stressed that we must be spiritually born again to *"see the kingdom of God."*

It should be every believer's goal and desire to be spirit-controlled; unfortunately, many never adequately learn to do this. They instead settle for being body-ruled Christians, thus cutting themselves off from the divine viewpoint and limiting themselves to the human perspective. A more common name for this is "carnal Christian."

There are degrees to this limiting condition, of course, and not every carnal Christian is frothing at the mouth with extreme iniquity, but they *are* body-ruled and therefore impeded from the divine viewpoint. Carnal Christians can become so hardened in heart by their sin that they naturally become hostile toward God and Christianity. As it is written:

> **The sinful mind is hostile to God. It does not submit to God's law, nor can it do so. [8]<u>Those controlled by the sinful nature</u> cannot please God.**
> **Romans 8:7-8**

Some flesh-ruled Christians become so hardened in heart by their sin that they end up denying Christ (!). This is the ultimate result of unrepentant and deceptive sin—it **destroys** your relationship with God. This is spiritual death—being dead to God—and explains why the Bible says: "The mind governed by the flesh is death" (Romans 8:6).

It should be pointed out that it takes time and effort to properly train the mind to habitually live according to the regenerated spirit with the help of the Holy Ghost. Most Christians will naturally need support from more mature brothers and sisters to learn to do this. In fact, the very reason God appoints and anoints spiritually mature believers to ministerial positions—like pastor, teacher or prophet—

is so that growing believers might be encouraged and equipped to successfully discern God's will for their lives, not to mention fulfill it (Ephesians 4:11-15).

The Positive Nature of the Flesh When Submitted to the Spirit

Allow me to add one important detail on this matter: When the mind is properly controlled by the spirit (which is, in turn, led by the indwelling Holy Spirit) the appetites and inclinations of the body actually become a positive force in a person's life. This is because the body is properly submitted to the spirit-led mind.

To illustrate, consider the sexual appetites of the body. If, in your mind, you choose to be flesh-ruled, the sexual appetite can be very destructive. For instance, unbridled sexual lust can lead you into fornication, adultery and perversion, resulting in broken relationships, broken families, illegitimate children, horrible diseases, prison and even death.

Yet when you choose to allow your mind to be spirit-led, your natural sexuality becomes a very positive and productive force in your life. There's nothing inherently wrong, for example, with the God-given male sex drive. The sex drive submitted to the spirit (with the help/leading of God's Spirit) will compel a man to find a suitable wife, physically love her and produce children.

Another good example would be anger. Anger stems from the carnal nature. We all realize that uncontrolled anger can be quite destructive, even provoking people to murder. Yet, when you choose to allow your mind to be spirit-led rather than flesh-ruled, anger can be utilized for righteous and productive purposes, rather than childish temper tantrums and worse.

A mother's anger over drunk driving is a fitting example: Her anger, properly submitted to the spirit, will compel her to seek social justice.

Or consider the biblical example of the Messiah when he got out a whip in righteous anger and drove everyone out of the Temple—overturning tables, scattering coins and yelling (John 2:13-17 & Mark 11:15-18). Needless to say, the common assumption that a good Christian must be a spineless doormat for other people is a lie. There's something called *tough* love and it's thoroughly biblical.

<u>8</u>

Core of the Mind: THE HEART

Many Bible passages speak of the human "heart," such as Mark 7:6 and 7:21. What exactly is the heart? And how does it fit into the biblical model of spirit, mind and flesh?

The Greek word for "heart" is *kardia (kar-DEE-ah),* which is where we get the English 'cardiac.' Like the English word 'heart,' *kardia* literally refers to the blood-pumping organ but figuratively to the **core thoughts or feelings of a person's being or mind** (Strong 39). E.W. Bullinger describes the heart as "**the seat and center** of man's personal life in which the distinctive character of the human manifests itself" (362).

The heart could therefore be best described as the core of the mind, the center of your being. It is part of the mind, but specifically the deepest, most central part, i.e. **the core**.

What's *in* your heart is determined by whether **your mind has** *decided* to live by the flesh or by the spirit. Jesus Christ said:

> **"The good man brings good things out of the good
> stored up in his heart, and the evil man brings evil
> things out of the evil stored up in his heart. For
> out of the overflow of the heart the mouth
> speaks."**
>
> **Luke 6:45**

If you, in your mind, *decide* to dwell on carnal thoughts, then carnal, negative, destructive things will naturally store up in your heart. If, on the other hand, you *choose* to dwell on spiritual thoughts—which means to "feed" them—then good, positive, productive things will store up in your heart.

The paraphrase of Proverbs 4:23 puts it like this: "**Be careful what you think, because your thoughts run your life**" (NCV). Take heed—truer words have never been spoken!

Here's a visual on how the heart fits into the biblical model of human nature:

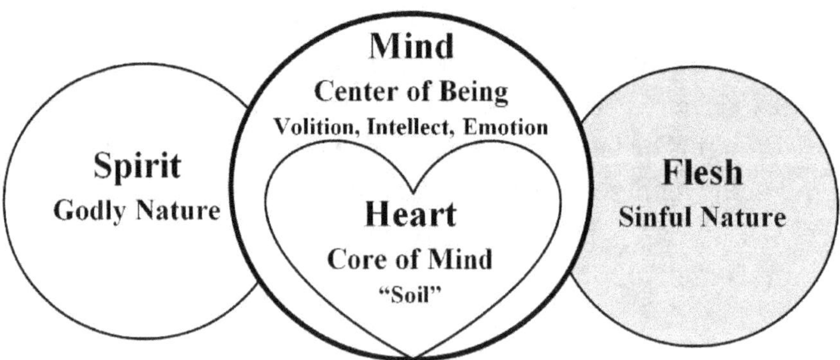

Notice that the heart is the core of your mind and is figuratively called "soil." Why? Because the Bible likens the heart to **soil** (Luke 8:15). Soil in the natural realm is a neutral substance that grows whatever seed is planted in it. This is the way it is with the soil of your heart, except that it grows non-physical "seeds," whether spiritual or *un*spiritual.

By "seeds" I mean thoughts, impulses, desires, images or impressions. Dwelling on these "seeds" waters them, so to speak, and thus enables them to nurture. In short, your meditation *feeds* them; and that is how they grow. Whatever is planted in your heart and grows there is what eventually fills your heart and produces the desires thereof. These desires of your heart then determine your character and therefore your actions, good or bad.

Has someone ever offended you and you dwelt on it so much that you made more of it than what it was? When the issue was finally resolved, you realized how you made a mountain out of a mole hill. How did this happen? Simple: You fed the offense with your thought life and thus it grew. As you kept thinking about it, the bigger the problem got. This principle goes into motion with any impulse you choose to focus on and give life to, whether it came from your spirit or the flesh.

The bottom line is that **you** *decide* what's stored up in your heart depending on whether you're governed by flesh or spirit.

I think it's important to point out that carnal and crazy thoughts will at times flash through your mind; yet this doesn't mean they're stemming from your heart. Having carnal and squirrely thoughts flash through the mind is natural to the human experience; in other words, if you're human, it happens. Sometimes you may even be bombarded with such impulses. These thoughts may originate from the flesh, unclean spirits, ungodly people, the environment you're exposed to, or otherwise, but just because such things flash through your mind it does not mean they're *in* your heart.

These thoughts *are not you*, and *are not originating from your heart;* but they can become *you* if you allow them to get lodged in your heart by dwelling on them and giving them life. Such thoughts should just be ignored or, if that doesn't work, taken "captive" and made "obedient to Christ," the Word of God (2 Corinthians 10:3-5). Otherwise, they will become a weed with the potential of growing into a big, ugly tree of destructive bad fruit, e.g. bitterness, immorality, frustration, sloth, depression, arrogance, abuse, gossip/slander, rage, etc.

'What About Jeremiah 17:9?'

This question refers to the well-known verse that says: "The heart *is* deceitful above all *things*, and desperately wicked: who can know it?" (KJV). You'll hear it quoted fairly often by sermonizers with the implication that the heart of *every* person is *always* deceitful and desperately wicked.

Yet the verse is referring **specifically** to the hardened hearts of the people of Judah *of that era* to whom Isaiah was prophesying. See Jeremiah 16:12, 17:1 and 18:12 for verification. So, to take Jeremiah 17:9 and apply it to *all* people throughout history is an example of taking a verse out of its context, which violates the hermeneutical rule 'context is king.'

Again, **Jesus Christ himself** plainly taught in Luke 6:45 that:

- A good person brings good things out of the good stored up in his/her heart.
- And an evil person brings evil things out of the evil stored up in his/her heart.

As such, a person's heart is not always automatically deceitful and wicked. It depends on the wisdom or folly of the individual in question and what they've allowed to grow in *their* heart.

Those who are wise understand the principle of the aforementioned proverb…

> **Be careful what you think,**
> **because your thoughts run your life.**
> **Proverbs 4:23** (NCV)

It reminds me of the old tale (commonly attributed to the Cherokee or another tribe) that goes like this:

> *There are two wolves inside you and they are always fighting. One is evil and the other good. Which wolf wins? The one you feed.*

9

YOUR RESURRECTION BODY

Even the most mature, spirit-controlled believer will fail to reach perfection as long as s/he dwells within a perishable flesh & blood body. Absolute escape from the sin nature will not be complete until the resurrection whereupon the redeemed will receive new glorified bodies:

> [35] But someone will ask, "How are the dead raised? With what kind of <u>body</u> will they come?"...
> [42b] The body that is sown is perishable, it is raised <u>imperishable</u>; [43] it is sown in dishonor, it is raised in <u>glory</u>; it is sown in weakness, it is raised in <u>power</u>; [44] it is sown a natural body, it is raised a <u>spiritual</u> body.
>
> **1 Corinthians 15:35, 42b-44**

This passage describes the new bodies that believers in Christ will receive at the resurrection of the righteous, which happens to take place in stages corresponding to the analogy of a biblical harvest:

- **Firstfruits** applies to Christ's resurrection (1 Corinthians 15:20-23).
- **The Main Harvest** takes place at the time of the Rapture (1 Thessalonians 4:13-17).
- **Gleanings** are relevant to the beginning and end of the Millennium (Leviticus 19:9-10).

All three together constitute the resurrection of the righteous. [7]

However, our focus here is verses 42-44 (quoted above). This passage contextually refers to spiritually alive believers, not spiritually dead people. The latter will of course be resurrected later in order to be judged and "Anyone whose name was not found written in the book of life was thrown into the lake of fire" (Revelation 20:11-15).

The text describes the new bodies of the redeemed as **imperishable, glorified, powerful** and **spiritual** in nature. Let's briefly consider what each of these means:

- **Imperishable** indicates that our resurrection bodies will not be able to perish. In short, we'll be immortal, which is one of the core benefits of the message of Christ (2 Timothy 1:10; John 3:36).
- **Glorified**: The Greek word for "glory" here is *doxa*, which means 'honor, renown; glory, an especially divine quality,

---

[7] If you find this intriguing and want more details, see chapter 11 of *SHEOL KNOW*, also available at the FOL site as the article *RESURRECTIONS: Firstfruits, Harvest & Gleanings.*

the unspoken manifestation of God, splendor.' In short, there will be nothing dishonorable about our resurrection bodies; they will reflect God's splendor in every way. After all, are we not *children* of God, *born* of Christ's seed? See John 1:12-13 and 1 John 3:9.

- **Powerful**: This word in the Greek is *dunamis (DOO-nah-miss)*, which is where we get the English dynamite. It means power, might, strength, force, energy. With our new resurrected bodies, we can say goodbye to the maladies that commonly mar our current ones, like fatigue, injury and disease. We'll be *invulnerable,* like Superman!

- **Spiritual**: This word in the Greek is *pneumatikos (nyoo-ma-tik-OSS)*, which obviously hails from the term for spirit, *pneuma.* Since spirit is polar opposite to the flesh or sinful nature (Galatians 5:17-23), this indicates that our resurrection bodies will not have a sinful nature and thus the proclivity to sin will be absent. You see, the flesh—the sinful nature—cannot inhabit the redeemed universe-to-come (2 Peter 3:13). Granting us such *spiritual* bodies is God's final measure in our obtaining freedom from sin. The power of sin and death will be "swallowed up in victory" (1 Corinthians 15:54-57)!

Here's another nugget to consider: The idea that our resurrection bodies will be spiritual, as well as physical, suggests that we'll be able to "fly" in these new bodies by floating in the air or "riding the wind." Christ was able to defy physical laws and walk on water by faith while in his mortal body (Matthew 14:22-33), how much more will we be able to do such things with *glorified, spiritual* bodies?

Lastly, the resurrected Messiah was able to appear seemingly from nowhere and disappear just as easily (Luke 24:31 & 24:36-37). How was he able to do this? Since his glorified body had a spiritual component, he likely entered into the spiritual dimension, which then gave him access to anywhere in the physical realm.

Speaking of which, although we cannot fully grasp now how wondrous life will be in these new resurrection bodies in the eternal age-to-come since we presently "see through a glass darkly," we can get an idea simply by observing what the Bible says about Christ after his resurrection. After all, we're going to receive the same type of glorified body he did seeing as how we're **co-heirs** with Christ" (Romans 8:17).

As such, we'll be able to walk through solid objects (John 20:26), instantly appear out of nowhere and disappear (Luke 24:31,36-37). You could say we'll be able to teleport at will. With this understanding, we'll no doubt be able to take "quantum leaps" to anywhere on the New Earth and Universe—including planets and galaxies millions of light-years away. Distances and space will no longer limit us.

I find this extremely invigorating and excitedly look forward to it (unlike the traditional concept of living on a cloud playing a harp forever).[8]

---

[8] For amazing insights on the nature of eternal life, see the Epilogue of *SHEOL KNOW* or check out the articles at the FOL site: *ETERNAL LIFE ("Heaven"): Questions & Answers* and *Eternal Life ("Heaven") — What Will It Be Like?*

<u>10</u>

SPIRITUAL DEATH
Leads to Absolute Death

The strongest proof that the born-again believer is spiritually *alive* to the LORD and, by extension, unredeemed people are spiritually *dead* to God, can be found in this passage:

> **You, however, are controlled not by the sinful nature but by the spirit, if the Spirit of God lives in you. And if anyone does not have the Spirit of Christ, he does not belong to Christ. ¹⁰ But <u>if Christ is in you</u>, your body is dead because of sin, yet <u>your spirit is alive</u> because of righteousness.**
> **Romans 8:9-10**

The key statement for our subject is verse 10: "If Christ is in you… your spirit is **alive**". The obvious implication is that, if the human spirit of a spiritually reborn believer is *alive*, the human spirit of an unregenerated person must be *dead*.

What exactly does this mean? Dead in what sense? Paul answers such questions here:

> **But whoever is <u>united with the Lord</u> is <u>one with him in spirit.</u>**
>
> **1 Corinthians 6:17**

This reveals that the unsaved person is *not* one with the Lord in spirit. In other words, s/he is dead to God and therefore separated from the Creator.

Being spiritually dead in this way is due to lacking *eternal* life *(zoe)*. Acts 17:25 plainly says that **God gives *all* people life** *(zoe)*, yet this refers to the *temporal* life *(zoe)* that is given to all humanity through Adam. *Eternal* life *(zoe)*, on the other hand, **is only available through Christ**, as verified by several clear passages, such as the popular John 3:16, and this verse:

> **but it has now been revealed through the appearing of our Savior, Christ Jesus, who has destroyed death and <u>has brought life and immortality to light through the gospel.</u>**
>
> **2 Timothy 1:10**

Are you getting this?

- Those who are spiritually dead only possess the **temporal** life *(zoe)* transferred to them via Adam.
- Such people are in desperate need of **eternal** life *(zoe)*, which is only available through the message of Christ (1 Corinthians 15:22).
- This is what the Christian gospel is all about and explains why it's such "Good News."

Spiritual Death, Physical Death and the Second Death

Those who are alive on Earth, but are spiritually dead, are destined to suffer two deaths—physical death and the second death. The "second death" takes place when an unredeemed person is condemned and discarded in the lake of fire (Revelation 20:11-15).

All of this data reveals that spiritual death is a *present* state in the lives of unredeemed people, as noted by Christ (John 5:24) and John (1 John 3:14). This explains why Paul described the believers in Ephesus and Colossae as being "dead in their sins" *before* they accepted the Lord (Ephesians 2:1; Colossians 2:13). These believers were spiritually dead *prior to* their rebirth in Christ.

This is in contrast to all the scriptural passages which clearly state that the second death—the literal destruction of soul and body in hell—is an experience that takes place in the future. Specifically, at the Great White Throne Judgment (Hebrews 10:26-27 & 10:31). In other words, the second death is not a present state but a future experience that will eventually occur, yet **only if** the individual foolishly fails to reconcile with God and receive the gracious gift of eternal life.

We see the contrast between spiritual death and the second death in Romans 8:10 and 8:13. The former verse is quoted at the beginning of this chapter and clearly implies that the spirit of an unsaved person is presently dead. Yet notice what Paul says about the second death a mere three verses later:

> **For if you live according to the sinful nature you <u>will</u> die; but if by the Spirit you put to death the misdeeds of the body, you will live.**
>
> **Romans 8:13**

Do you see the clear contrast between spiritual death and the second death here? Paul says that people who choose to live according to the flesh will eventually have to reap the wages of their actions and die. This is the second death—absolute destruction of soul and body in Gehenna, the lake of fire. As it is written:

> **"Do not be afraid of those who kill the body but cannot kill the soul. Rather, be afraid of the One who can destroy both soul and body in hell."**
> **Matthew 10:28**

This, again, is a future event, not a present state.

So, **spiritual death ultimately results in absolute death**. That's why God sent his Son so that "whoever believes in him shall **not perish** but have eternal life" (John 3:16).

The third chapter of John ends with an insightful rephrasing of this:

> **Whoever believes in the Son <u>has eternal life</u>, but whoever rejects the Son <u>will not see life</u>, for God's wrath remains on them.**
> **John 3:36**

Why won't they see eternal life? Because they're **spiritually dead** and the only life they have is the temporal life transferred to them through Adam. They need born-anew of the second Adam, Jesus Christ:

> **For as in Adam <u>all die</u>, so in Christ all will be <u>made alive</u>.**
> **1 Corinthians 15:22**

(See the <u>Appendix</u> for further insights on Spiritual Death).

<u>11</u>

THE UNREDEEMED
and Their Human Spirit

The material we've been covering so far brings up an interesting question: Can a person who is spiritually dead to God train his/her mind to live according to their (unregenerated) human spirit? Absolutely, and this explains the many unbelievers we run into regularly who display noble characteristics even though their spirit isn't regenerated and therefore isn't united with God.

We have to remember that Adam didn't eat of the tree of the knowledge of evil; he ate of the tree of the knowledge of *good* and evil (Genesis 2:17; 3:11-12). This, incidentally, was the origin of the condition of spiritual death, discussed last chapter.[9]

The entire human race, as Adam's descendants, therefore possesses the capacity for both good and evil. However, even though we have the capacity for good, Adam passed on to humanity a sin nature or flesh—the carnal proclivity to rebel against good, aka God's

---

[9] Also see the <u>Appendix</u>.

righteous laws, which are universally known to people around the globe (Romans 1:32; 2:14-15; 7:12).

As already determined, this sinful nature is largely a condition of the body, but negatively affects the rest of one's being as well, specifically the mind, depending on how much the individual has acquiesced to the desires of the flesh.

Adam & Eve's fallen condition has been passed on to all of those born of them, which means the entire human race. As such, the unbeliever's spirit is **rendered dead to God**—incapable of connecting with the Creator, unless it is reborn of the Holy Spirit via the seed of Christ, as noted in 1 John 3:9. The word for "seed" in that verse happens to be the Greek word for sperm, *sperma*.

Because Adam ate of the tree of the knowledge of both good and evil, most people who are not spiritually regenerated are a mishmash of spiritual and carnal qualities; that is, they possess both good and bad traits.[10] Only a relatively small number of unbelievers could be designated as *wholly* wicked; and even they no doubt have *some* good qualities. (Although I sometimes wonder how "good" people would be if there were no human laws to keep them in check.[11] In other words, if they could "get away" with stealing, raping or murdering, would they do it? Only God knows their hearts).

This explains the unbelievers we regularly come across who seem quite developed in character. Even though they're not spiritually

---

[10] Spiritually regenerated believers are also a mishmash of both good and bad traits; I'm not suggesting otherwise, but our topic here is individuals who are *not* spiritually reborn.

[11] If people don't fear God's law—that is, universal moral law—the only law they have left to fear is human law; but if there's no human law to constrain their lower impulses (or they're not held *accountable to* that law), they would naturally have nothing to fear. This would be the ultimate test of character.

united with God, they appear to be humble, intelligent, loving, positive, moral, compassionate, etc. Such people have somehow trained their minds to live according to their spirit which, even though it's dead to God and thus in dire need of regeneration, is still the facet of their being that inclines toward what is positive, productive and godly, as opposed to the flesh which veers toward negativity, destruction and perversion.

There's always some training or discipline that enables individuals to do this. It could simply be the result of how they were raised, in which case they were trained by their parents or mentors to be loving and moral. It could also be the result of their exposure and submission to various "disciplines." Some examples include religion, meditation and martial arts, as well as generally positive philosophies, such as <u>Sciencefictionology</u>.[12]

Such disciplines could be considered good in some ways since they inspire folks to be the best that they can be, yet **they ultimately fail to solve the sin problem and reconcile people to their Creator**. For this reason, they have the potential for harm as these disciplines can delude people into thinking they can attain righteousness by their own works *without* spiritual regeneration and God. This notion is rooted in pride and arrogance, sins the LORD "hates" (Proverbs 8:13) (also see14:12 and 16:25).

The message of the Bible is that humankind is cursed with a sin nature and a spirit that is dead to God. Hence, no amount of human effort to attain righteousness can adequately remove our sinfulness and reconcile us to the Almighty. As noted in chapter <u>6</u>, salvation through human effort is impossible (Matthew 19:26).

---

[12] This is simply an amusing reference to Scientology in light of its mastermind, L. Ron Hubbard, being a renowned sci-fi author.

Although it is certainly commendable that a person makes a conscious decision to live by his/her spirit, in a sense it's all flesh to God because the infection of sin has tainted the human spirit and rendered it dead. It is incapable of doing what it was originally designed to do—enable the person to commune with God and supply eternal life. Theologians refer to this state as "total depravity." This doesn't mean that human beings are as bad as we could possibly be apart from redemption in Christ, but that we are unable to contribute to our salvation in any way because we are spiritually dead in our fallen condition.

The obvious exception is **humble repentance & faith** in response to the awesome message of Christ (Acts 20:21; Mark 1:15; James 4:6). Repentance & faith are two sides of the same coin and are, unsurprisingly, **the first two** of the six basic doctrines of Christianity, as observed by Hebrews 6:1-2.

It should be added that there is another danger in attempting to live out of the unregenerated spirit (beyond the pitfall of pride). Anyone who does so will become increasingly in tune with the spiritual realm. The problem with this is that there are both good and evil spirits. If a person's spirit is disunited from God, it stands to reason that the spiritual realm they're more prone to get in tune with would *not* be of God.

Unless intercessory prayer is made on their behalf—thereby "loosing" the Holy Spirit to draw them to God—they are vulnerable to the deception and misleading of impure spirits. This is how false religions and philosophies develop. Their message is always the same: There's *another way* to the Creator besides the gospel of reconciliation through Christ (2 Corinthians 5:18-21).

Perhaps the ultimate satanic deception is that humankind can somehow attain righteousness apart from God's gift of righteousness in Christ (Romans 5:17). As already pointed out, this notion—that we can be good without God, that we don't need our Creator—is rooted in human arrogance. Consequently, the human attempt to be righteous apart from God is a fleshly stench to the all-knowing LORD who knows the secrets and motivations of the heart.

The popular message today is that there are many paths to God, none superior to any other, so what I'm teaching here will be rejected by those who embrace the spirit of this age. The bottom line is that God loves the whole world in an active sense and has thus provided a way to spiritual regeneration, reconciliation and eternal life. Let's be wise and go with **God's way** (biblical, Spirit-led Christianity), and reject the **human way** (religion). Amen?

So, to answer the question, can persons who are spiritually unregenerated learn to live out of their human spirit and consequently produce good works and develop in character? Certainly. This is commendable, but whatever discipline they follow ultimately fails to heal their fallen condition and reconcile them to the Almighty. This is "total depravity."

<u>12</u>

"SPIRIT" and "THE BREATH OF LIFE"

Take a deep breath (no pun intended) because this is where the topic gets a little complex due to the limitations of human language, which I'll elaborate on in the next chapter. Hang in there and I promise you everything will make perfect sense.

In our study so far, we've determined that the human spirit is the facet of human nature that is opposed to the flesh. It is the part of your being that compels you toward what is positive & godly and inspires the desire to connect with your Creator. It should be pointed out that in certain contexts 'spirit' refers to "the breath of life." The breath of life could also be referred to as the spirit of life because "breath" is translated from the same Hebrew and Greek words for "spirit"—*ruwach* and *pneuma* respectively.

The "breath of life" describes the human spirit on the most basic level as separate from mind and body: The human spirit is essentially a breath of life from God, keeping in mind that "God is spirit" (John 4:24). As such, **the breath of life is not your being; it**

is the spiritual lifeforce from God that gives consciousness to your being. In other words, **the very reason you have consciousness is because of the breath of life, but the breath of life is not your consciousness**.

We could draw a parallel to the human body. The body is the facet of human nature that enables your being to dwell in the physical realm. It is indeed a part of your being, but it is not your consciousness, rather it enables your consciousness to dwell in the physical realm. Separate from spirit and mind, the body is just a carcass, a slab of nonliving flesh. This is what the body is on the most basic level separate from spirit and mind. Similarly, **separate from mind and body, the human spirit is simply a breath of life from God**.

We've discovered from the Scriptures that the mind is the center of one's being. Your mind has the power of will and therefore makes decisions. It is also the emotional and intellectual seat of your being; you therefore feel and reason with your mind.

The breath of life gives consciousness to the mind, the center of your being. The breath of life—or spirit of life—could thus be described as **the animating spiritual lifeforce from God**. You see, the human being consists of material and immaterial facets, physical and non-physical. Your immaterial being is your mind or disembodied soul. We could describe the mind as spiritual in nature and substance. **Your spiritual being (mind) requires a spiritual breath of life to live just as your physical being requires a physical breath of life to live.** In fact, "breath of life" often refers simultaneously to both spiritual and physical breath in the Scriptures. This will be made clear as we continue.

The Bible reveals that animals have a breath of life just as human beings do. We could therefore say that animals have a spirit, yet only in the sense that they have a breath of life. They certainly don't have a spirit in the sense that they possess a godly nature. The human being, as the LORD's highest order of living creature on Earth, was created in God's image (Genesis 1:26-27). Our spiritual makeup therefore prompts a desire to connect or commune with God and drives us toward goodness and productivity. The human spirit is endowed with this "godly nature." This is a fact whether the spirit is regenerated or not.

All the passages we've looked at up to this point on the human spirit refer to this godly nature, such as Proverbs 20:27 and Matthew 26:41. The passages we'll focus on now refer to…

The Breath of Life

Two words are used for 'breath' in the phrase "breath of life" in the Hebraic Scriptures:

- *Ruwach (ROO-ahk),* which corresponds to the Greek *pneuma (NYOO-mah).*
- *Neshamah (nesh-aw-MAW).*

Like *ruwach/pneuma, neshamah* can refer to "breath," "wind" or "spirit."[13]

So *ruwach/pneuma* and *neshamah* are basically interchangeable words. Let's turn to the book of Genesis to observe biblical support for this:

---

[13] Although *neshamah* rarely refers to the human spirit's godly nature, it does so in Proverbs 20:27.

66

> **Pairs of all creatures that have the <u>breath</u> *(ruwach)* of life in them came to Noah and entered the ark.**
>
> **Genesis 7:15**

> **Everything on dry land that had the <u>breath</u> *(neshamah)* of life in its nostrils died. [23] Every living thing on the face of the earth was wiped out; <u>men and animals</u>… Only Noah was left, and those with him in the ark.**
>
> **Genesis 7:22-23**

The first text refers to the animals that accompanied Noah to his colossal vessel. They had "the breath of life." The second text refers to every living thing on Earth that had "the breath of life" and died as a result of the flood—human and animal. This is evidence that *ruwach* and *neshamah* are used interchangeably in the Bible.

These two passages clearly show that animals as well as humans have the breath of life. This proves that the breath of life cannot be a reference to the human spirit's "godly nature" because the animal spirit possesses no such nature. It is this factor that distinguishes animalkind from humankind: The human spirit possesses a godly nature whereas the animal spirit is merely a breath of life, an animating lifeforce from the Creator. Because the human spirit is endowed with a godly nature, people possess an inherent inclination toward goodness, productivity and godliness; which is contrasted by a carnal nature, the inclination toward destruction, negativity and evil.

Animals of course have neither a spirit (godly nature) nor flesh (sinful nature). Animals are instinctual creatures that live and act by instinct. Their actions are therefore neither good nor evil, unlike human beings.

Interestingly, the same Hebrew and Greek words for 'soul' *(nephesh/psuche)* are used in reference to animals in the Bible. Translators usually render *nephesh/psuche* as "creature(s)" or "thing" in such cases, rather than "soul(s)." See for example Genesis 1:20,24 and Revelation 8:9 & 16:3.[14]

In these contexts, 'soul' *(nephesh/psuche)* must be defined in its broadest sense as "a living being." Like humans, animals are living beings or living souls but, unlike humans, they lack both a spiritual dimension and carnal dimension. In other words, animals are living souls but they do not have a spirit or flesh—a godly nature or sinful nature. Because they lack the higher spiritual dimension inherent to people, animals are unaware of the existence of God and lack the ability or desire to commune with the Creator.

In light of this, whenever the Hebrew word for "spirit"—*ruwach*—is used in reference to animals in the Scriptures, we know it always refers to the breath of life, the animating lifeforce of the Almighty, which enables them to live. This is the extent and limit of their spiritual dimension. Here's support for this:

> **"I** [God] **am going to bring floodwaters on the earth to destroy all life under the heavens, every <u>creature</u>** *(nephesh)* **that has the <u>breath</u>** *(ruwach)* **of life in it. Everything on earth will perish."**
>
> **Genesis 6:17**

This verse describes both animals and humans as *nephesh* ("creatures"), which is the Hebrew word for 'soul'; and then goes on to state that these creatures (souls) have the "breath of life." "Breath" here is the Hebrew word for 'spirit,' *ruwach*. Since *ruwach* is used in reference to both animals and humans, we know it refers

---

[14] This is covered in more detail in chapter <u>4</u> of *HELL KNOW*.

to the breath of life, the animating lifeforce from the Almighty that sustains all living creatures. It does not refer to what we understand as the human spirit's godly nature, the human inclination toward goodness and godliness. Animals, once again, do not have a spirit as such. Keep in mind that "breath" in this passage simultaneously refers to physical breath, which we'll look at in a moment.

All of this is made clear in this passage from Psalm 104, which contextually refers to animals of all kinds (see verses 17-25) and, in fact, includes human beings as well (verse 23):

> **Thou** [God] **dost take away their <u>spirit</u>** *(ruwach)*,
> **they expire.**
> **And return to their dust.**
> **³⁰Thou dost send forth thy <u>spirit</u>** *(ruwach),*
> **they are created;**
>
> **Psalm 104:29b-30a** (NASB)

This plainly shows that all animals are created by a *ruwach* from God (verse 30) and **expire** when God takes this *ruwach* away.[15] It's not rocket science.

Animals do not have a spirit in the sense of a godly nature as humans do, but both animals and humans have a spirit in the sense of a breath of life that animates and sustains them. And that's what *ruwach* in this passage refers to. This is why most other translations do not translate *ruwach* as "spirit" in verse 29, but as "breath" (see, for example, the NIV, KJV and NRSV).

---

[15] Many translations translate *ruwach* in verse 30 as "Spirit" (capitalized) giving the impression that the verse refers to God's Spirit; but let's remember that there is no capitalization in the original Hebrew. With this understanding, it is clear that *ruwach* in verse 30 refers to the same *ruwach* referred to in verse 29, that is, the breath of life—the spiritual animating lifeforce of the Almighty. See the NRSV rendition of this text and the accompanying footnote for support.

Now consider this passage:

> **Surely the fate of human beings is like that of the animals; the same fate awaits them both: As one dies, so dies the other. All have the same <u>breath</u>** *(ruwach)***; humans have no advantage over animals. Everything is meaningless.**
>
> **Ecclesiastes 3:19**

This is an enlightening verse. It says that both humans and animals have "the same *ruwach*." While there is the possibility that *ruwach* in this verse is referring to mere physical breath, we will see why this conclusion must be ruled out. Rather, *ruwach* here refers to the breath of life—the animating spiritual lifeforce from God—and not to what we understand as the human spirit's godly nature. This is obvious for two reasons:

1. The text plainly states that both humans and animals have the same *ruwach*. Since animals don't have a spirit in the sense that humans have a spirit, *ruwach* in this passage must refer to the breath of life because we know from other passages that both humans and animals are sustained by a "breath of life."
2. Notice that the text says both humans and animals have "the **same** *ruwach*." All creatures have the same animating lifeforce from the Almighty—the same spiritual breath *(ruwach)* of life. This *ruwach* of life is a depersonalized life force.

In other words, the breath of life in this context **is the spiritual lifeforce that gives life to the person, but is not itself the person; it gives consciousness to the being but is not the consciousness of the being.** It's comparable to electricity that lights up a lamp: The electricity enables the lamp to have light, but the electricity is not the lamp's light. Furthermore, when the lamp is unplugged and loses its source of electricity, its light expires. The same is true in regards to God's breath *(ruwach)* of life. As the aforementioned Psalm states, "Thou [God] dost take away their spirit *(ruwach)*, they expire" (104:29 NASB).

Two verses later, in Ecclesiastes 3:21, Solomon speculates on where the spirit of a person and the spirit of an animal go after death: "Who knows if the spirit *(ruwach)* of man rises upward and if the spirit *(ruwach)* of the animal goes down into the earth?" It's once again obvious that *ruwach* here refers to the spiritual breath of life and this is why the NASB translates *ruwach* as "breath" in this passage (even though most others translate it as "spirit"). This verse gives evidence that Solomon was not referring to mere physical oxygen—in both this passage and verse 19 above—since it would be ludicrous to argue whether oxygen "rises upward" or "goes down into the earth."

What then was Solomon trying to express by this question? He was simply pointing out that, from a *purely natural viewpoint* (that is, "under the sun"—which is the perspective of Ecclesiastes), human beings appear to be little different than animals and both ultimately perish from this plane of existence. In reality, however, the human soul, unlike the animal soul, is created in the image of its Creator and thus possesses a higher spiritual dimension enabling us to be aware of our Creator and desire to commune.

<u>13</u>

"THE BREATH OF LIFE": God's Animating Life Force

Let's now return to "the creation text" with focus on how the breath of life figures into God's creation of human beings:

> **The LORD formed the man from the dust of the ground and breathed into his nostrils the <u>breath</u> (neshamah) of life, and the man became a living <u>being</u> (nephesh).**
>
> Genesis 2:7

This shows that God formed the body of man out of the essential chemical elements of the Earth and breathed into his nostrils the breath of life and thus he became "a **living** soul." In chapter <u>3</u> we saw that *nephesh*—the Hebrew word for "being" or "soul"—can refer more specifically to the body in certain contexts. You see, a body without the breath of life is a **dead** soul *(nephesh)* whereas a body with the breath of life is a **living** soul *(nephesh)*. As such, it's obvious that it is the breath of life—God's spiritual lifeforce—that animates the mind or soul and enables us to actually live. (The body,

72

once again, is merely the facet of human nature that enables us to function in the physical realm). Elihu makes this clear:

> **"If it were his** [God's] **intention**
> **and he withdrew his <u>spirit</u>** *(ruwach)* **and**
> **<u>breath</u>** *(neshamah),*
> [15]**all humanity would perish together**
> **and mankind would return to the dust."**
>
> **Job 34:14-15** [16]

We see here further proof that *ruwach* and *neshamah* are used interchangeably; although in this particular passage *ruwach* would refer to God's *spiritual* breath—his animating lifeforce—and *neshamah* would refer to *physical* breath. You see, God's spiritual breath of life animates the mind (disembodied soul) which in turn animates the body; and the body is physically sustained by physical breath.

The *ruwach* breath of life could be viewed as the spiritual counterpart to the physical *neshamah* breath of life. Just as your physical body needs air to live and function, so your disembodied

---

[16] Elihu's words are reliable, as he appears to be a type of Christ. The biblical support for this is as follows: **1.** Elihu claimed to be "perfect in knowledge" (Job 36:4) whereas only the LORD is "perfect in knowledge" (37:16); God, as well as Job and his three friends, would have certainly rebuked Elihu for this seemingly arrogant statement if, in fact, it was not true. **2.** Elihu's questioning rebuke to Job in 37:14-23 coincides with the LORD's questioning rebuke to Job in chapters 38-41. **3.** God rebuked Job because he "spoke words without knowledge" (38:1-2), as did Elihu (35:16). **4.** Job would not or could not respond to Elihu's rebuke (as he was sure to do with each of his three friends). **5.** God rebuked Job (chapters 38-41) and his three friends—Eliphaz, Zophar and Bildad (42:7-9)—for their error, but He never rebukes or even mentions Elihu. *Apparently* Elihu was right and just in God's eyes. **6.** Like Christ, Elihu acted as the mediator between God and man: Elihu spoke *after* Job and his three friends and *before* God (mediating between the two). **7.** Elihu righteously showed no partiality and refused to flatter (32:21).

soul—your mind—needs spiritual breath to live and function. Just as physical breath is not a person, neither is spiritual breath a person. Greek and Hebrew scholar, W.E. Vine, helps us to understand this relationship between the breath of life, the disembodied soul (mind) and the body:

> **The spirit** *may be recognized as the life principle bestowed on man by God,* **the soul** *as the resulting life constituted in the individual,* **the body** *being the material organism animated by* **soul and spirit** *(589[68]).*

Keep in mind that when Vine refers to "spirit" he's referring to the breath of life and when he refers to "soul" he's referring to the mind.

Secondly, we see further proof that, if God withdrew his breath of life, all humanity would perish and our bodies would decay back to dust, which is evident in this Psalm passage:

> **Do not put your trust in princes,**
> **in human beings, who cannot save.**
> **⁴When their <u>spirit</u>** *(ruwach)* **departs, they return**
> **to the ground;**
> **on that very day their plans come to nothing.**
> **Psalm 146:3-4**

Ruwach ("spirit") here refers to the breath of life. When the breath of life departs, the human body merely decays into the ground.

At Death, the Breath of Life Goes Back to God

So, what happens to the breath of life when a person (or animal) dies? It merely goes back to God from whence it came. As it is written:

> **Remember him** [God]—**before the silver cord is**
>   **severed,**
>   **and the golden bowl is broken;**
>   **before the pitcher is shattered at the spring,**
>   **and the wheel broken at the well,**
> **⁷and the dust returns to the ground it came from,**
>   **and the <u>spirit</u>** *(ruwach)* **returns to God who**
>   **gave it.**
>
> **Ecclesiastes 12:6-7**

Verse 6 uses various metaphors to encourage us to think of our Creator before death inevitably overtakes us. Verse 7 then explains what happens to the human body and the breath of life when we die. The breath of life, again, is the spiritual lifeforce from God that animates the human being and makes it a *living* soul. The breath of life gives life to the mind/spirit in the human body. When an unredeemed person dies this depersonalized lifeforce merely returns to the Creator who gave it.

This is further proof that the breath of life is not just physical oxygen. When people die their physical breath simply returns to the atmosphere; there's no need for it to return to God. Yet when we understand that the breath of life is a *spiritual* breath—an animating lifeforce from God—it then makes sense that it returns to its source, the Giver of Life from which all life flows (Psalm 36:9).

The fact that the breath of life returns to God is evident in Elihu's previously quoted statement: "If it were his intention and he withdrew his spirit and breath all humanity would perish together and mankind would return to the dust" (Job 34:14-15). The statement "If God withdrew his spirit and breath" implies that the breath of life will simply return to God who gave it.

Keep in mind, of course, that Solomon wrote this some ten centuries *before* Jesus Christ died for our sins and was raised for our justification and, in the process, "destroyed death and brought life and immortality to light through the gospel" (2 Timothy 1:10). Consequently, believers who are born-again of the imperishable **seed** of Christ[17] don't have to fear death since Yeshua destroyed him who holds the power of death—the devil (Hebrews 2:14-15). When we physically perish, we are ushered into the presence of the LORD, Praise God! This is verified by Philippians 1:21-24, 2 Corinthians 5:8, Revelation 6:9-11 and 7:9-17 beyond any shadow of doubt.[18]

Bear in mind, however, that this is only the "intermediate state" of believers between physical death and bodily resurrection, and is therefore a *temporary* condition. As far as eternity goes, we are "looking forward to a new heaven and a new earth, the (eternal) home of righteousness" (2 Peter 3:13; see also Revelation 21-22).[19]

The Limitations of Human Language

Getting back to "the breath of life," some readers may feel that I've gone into this issue a little too deeply, but it's important for us to understand that the Hebrew and Greek words for "spirit" *(ruwach* and *pneuma)* can refer to *either* the human spirit or the breath of life in passages pertaining to human nature in the Scriptures. The specific verse and context will determine which of these *ruwach* and *pneuma* refer. If we assume that *ruwach* and *pneuma* always refer to the human spirit, the part of human nature that is opposed to the

---

[17] Remember, "seed" is translated from the Greek word for sperm in 1 John 3:9.

[18] For even further evidence, see chapter 10 of *SHEOL KNOW,* which is also available at the FOL site as the article *The Believer's INTERMEDIATE STATE (Between Physical Death and Bodily Resurrection).*

[19] Check out the Epilogue of *SHEOL KNOW* for more details; or the article *ETERNAL LIFE ("Heaven"): Questions & Answers* at the FOL site.

flesh, then the Scriptures can become very confusing. For instance, we would have to conclude that animals have a spirit just like humans have a spirit. Yet, we must understand that when God inspired people to write the Scriptures by his Holy Spirit (2 Peter 1:20-21) he was limited to flawed human language.

No human language is an exact science. Language is indeed a wondrous human creation, but it often makes little sense. We saw proof of this in chapter <u>3</u> where it was shown that the Hebrew word for "soul," *nephesh,* can refer to a dead body, a living whole person (spirit, mind and body), or the immaterial facet of human nature (mind & spirit). To further confuse the issue, *nephesh* most often refers to "life" in the Bible. Needless to say, the definition of *nephesh* depends on the passage and its context. So it is with the Hebrew and Greek words for "spirit."

The Greek *Pneuma* in Reference to the Breath of Life

Let us now turn our attention to the New Testament and observe occasions where the Greek *pneuma* obviously refers to the breath of life and not to the human spirit.

The following verse from Revelation is talking about God's anointed two witnesses who were killed by "the beast" and laid dead in the street for three and a half days:

> **But after three and a half days a <u>breath</u>** *(pneuma)*
> **of life from God entered them, and they stood on**
> **their feet, and terror struck those who saw them.**
> **Revelation 11:11**

The Greek word translated as "breath" here, *pneuma,* obviously refers to the breath of life—God's animating life force—and not to the human spirit as described earlier in this study. The breath of life animates the mind—the disembodied soul—which in turn animates the body. The way this verse describes how God resurrects these two people coincides with how he gave life to Adam (Genesis 2:7), as well as how he miraculously brought to life a bunch of dry bones and flesh in Ezekiel 37:1-14 (a vision that the LORD gave Ezekiel).

Pneuma likely refers to the breath of life in this popular passage as well:

> **As the body without the <u>spirit</u>** *(pneuma)* **is dead, so faith without works is dead.**
>
> **James 2:26**

In light of the afore-cited texts, it makes sense to regard *pneuma* here as a reference to the breath of life—the animating life force from God. If it's not a reference to the breath of life, then we would have to conclude that it refers to the entire immaterial facet of human nature, spirit and mind (which is W.E. Vine's interpretation [593]).

It makes little difference however, as it is God's breath of life that animates this immaterial facet of human nature which, in turn, animates the body.

<u>14</u>

THE DEFINITION
of Human Nature

In light of all the scriptural data we've examined, human nature could best be defined as such: **The HUMAN BEING is <u>a living soul</u> consisting of <u>spirit</u>, <u>mind</u> and <u>body</u> animated by <u>a breath of life</u> from God**. Here's a diagram to visualize this:

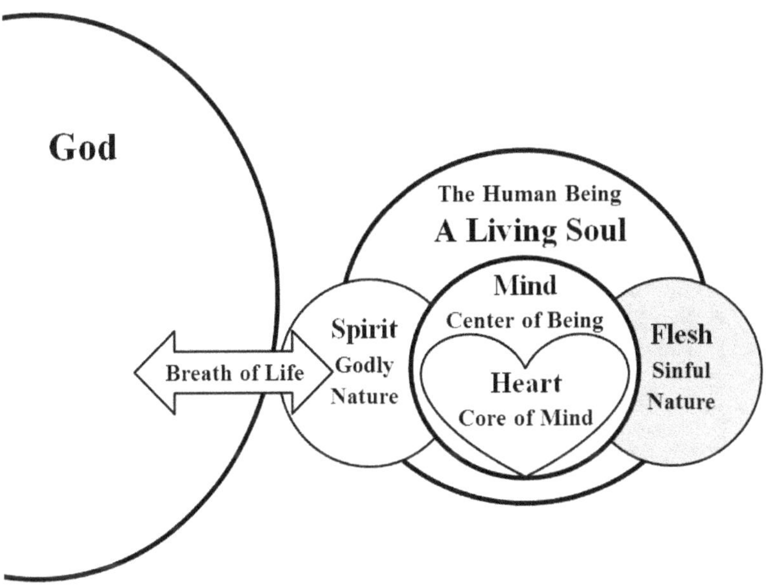

Someone wrote me and asked why the human body isn't featured in this diagram. Yet it *is* included: The body could be viewed as the largest circle labeled "The Human Being: A Living Soul." Meanwhile the three smaller circles—"Spirit," "Mind" and "Flesh"—relay what's going on *inside* the individual, which is the meat & potatoes of the topic.

Another way of looking at is that the largest circle—"A Living Soul"—refers to the whole individual—and the three smaller circles are what the human being consists of, with the body represented by the "Flesh" circle (seeing as how the Greek words for body—*soma* and *sarx*—can refer to either the physical body or the sinful nature, depending on context).

Closing Word

The topic of human nature is a little bit more detailed and sometimes complicated than I like to go into in my works, which explains why there's been so much confusion and misunderstanding on the topic in Church history. However, by looking at all the key words and their definitions pertaining to context—soul, spirit, mind, body, flesh, heart and breath of life—all the pieces of the scriptural puzzle come together and make sense.

More than that, the truth sets you free as you learn that the flesh or sinful nature is the proverbial "beast inside," which every human being has. Its impulses must be recognized and denied (or, better yet, **counted dead by faith**, in light of Romans 6:11), *not* fed and acted on. The world decries this as "repression," but it's actually a healthy practice.

Spiritual regeneration is the first step to walking free of the flesh, followed by renewing your mind (Romans 12:2) and learning to be spirit-controlled rather than flesh-ruled, with the help of the indwelling Holy Spirit. This is "walking in the spirit" (Galatians 5:16), also known as "participating in the divine nature" (2 Peter 1:4) or "clothing yourself in Christ" (Romans 13:14).

Once you understand these things, you can share them with others so they too can walk in the true freedom of biblical Christianity, as it is written:

> **"So if the Son sets you free, you will be free indeed."**
>
> **John 8:36**

> **It is for freedom that Christ has set us free. Stand firm, then, and do not let yourselves be burdened again by a yoke of slavery.**
>
> **Galatians 5:1**

> **because through Christ Jesus the law of the Spirit who gives life has set you free from the law of sin and death.**
>
> **Romans 8:2**

<u>Appendix</u>

Further Insights on
SPIRITUAL DEATH

As always with heavy theological topics like this, it's best to go to what the Word of Truth says (2 Timothy 2:15). Keeping in mind the 'law of first mention,' the concept of spiritual death is initially breached at the beginning of the book of Genesis:

> **And the LORD God commanded the man, "You are free to eat from any tree in the garden; [17]but you must not eat from the tree of the knowledge of good and evil, for when you eat from it you will <u>certainly die</u>** *(tamut muth).***"**
>
> **Genesis 2:16-17**

"Certainly die" in verse 17 is translated from two forms of the Hebrew verb for death, *muth*.[20] A more literal translation of the verse would be: "but you must not eat from the tree of the knowledge of good and evil, for when you eat of it, **dying, you will die**" (which is

---

[20] There are various spellings in transliteration; *muwth* is another.

essentially how the Young's Literal Translation renders it). In other words, the very day Adam sinned, part of his being died, leading to his eventual demise.

Muth always indicates that something has died or will die. It does not mean "separation" as some claim. If God meant to warn Adam that he would "separate," he would have used the Hebrew word *badal (bah-DAHL)*. So, what died? Adam's immortal nature. In other words, he lost his eternal life.

Hence, spiritual death means that **the human spirit is disconnected from God because it lacks eternal life**. If the human spirit is dead to God, it is impossible to have a *relationship* since the human spirit is the facet through which the person 'connects' with the LORD. As Jesus said: "**God is spirit**, and his worshipers must worship ***in spirit*** and in truth" (John 4:24).

Put another way, if a person is spiritually dead it is impossible to know and worship God in spirit. Why? Because they're spiritually disconnected from the Creator. Since they're spiritually dead they are separate from God, but 'dead' doesn't mean "separation"; rather, separation from the LORD is the ***result of*** being spiritually dead. Spiritually reborn believers, by contrast, are one with the Lord in spirit (1 Corinthians 6:17) because they are spiritually alive and possess eternal life (Romans 8:10; 1 John 5:11-12).

This can be observed in the fact that Adam & Eve hid from the LORD immediately *after* suffering spiritual death (Genesis 3:8-10). This condition robbed humanity of guilt-free access into the presence of God and the precious communion thereof.

Paul also spoke of spiritual death when he said: "Once I was alive apart from the law; but when the commandment came, sin sprang to life and I died" (Romans 7:9). This alludes to the age of accountability, which is the age that the LORD holds people accountable to sin. Have you ever run into a family where the parents are heavily involved in sin, like drugs, crime or sexual immorality, yet their kids are bright-eyed and bushy-tailed? Regardless of the moral degeneracy of their parents, the children have the sparkle of life in their eyes! It's incredible. Why is this? Because they're spiritually alive.[21]

The condition of spiritual death is passed on from Adam to everyone born into this world (Romans 5:12). Thus, anyone past the age of accountability will only experience **two deaths**—physical death and the "second death." In other words, spiritual death results in two inevitable deaths—physical death and the second death, the latter being eternal death, aka literal everlasting destruction (Matthew 10:28; Hebrews 10:26-27 & 10:31). Thankfully, no one *has* to suffer the second death and that's what makes the gospel of Christ such Good News (Romans 6:23; Revelation 2:11).

How Does "Original Sin" Relate to Spiritual Death?

To understand the condition of spiritual death, it is necessary to grasp, as already noted, that it is the spiritual side of human nature that actually unites with God. "Original sin" is the reason this capacity does not exist in those who are spiritually dead. The doctrine of original sin of course suggests that humanity's fallen nature—our inclination to commit sin and the corresponding alienation from our Creator—was naturally passed on to all of us by our primeval parents, Adam & Eve.

---

[21] See the article *What Is the "AGE OF ACCOUNTABILITY"?* at the FOL site for details.

In order for a person's spirit to unite with God, he or she needs to be spiritually regenerated. This explains why Yeshua taught that our spirit must be "born again" for us to "see the kingdom of God" (John 3:3-8) Those who are spiritually reborn "cross over from death to life" (John 5:24; 1 John 3:14). In other words, they transfer from a state of spiritual death to a state of spiritual life.

The "second death," by contrast, is a *future event* entailing the complete destruction of soul and body in the lake of fire (Revelation 20:11-15). So, the condition of **spiritual death ultimately results in the second death**, which is an **absolute death** (James 5:20; Luke 19:27).

I want to stress that the awesome message of Christ is all about fixing the condition of spiritual death and its repercussions by redeeming humanity through the substitutionary death of our Lord (1 Peter 2:24; Isaiah 53:6; John 3:16).

<u>Bibliography</u>

(A person's inclusion in this list does not equal wholesale endorsement)

Benner, Jeff. *The Ancient Hebrew Lexicon of the Bible.* College Station: Virtualbookworm Publishing, 2005

Brown, Francis/Driver, S.R./Briggs, Charles A. *Brown-Driver-Briggs Lexicon.* Peabody: Hendrickson Publishers, 1994

Bullinger, Ethelbert W. *A Critical Lexicon and Concordance to the English and Greek New Testament.* Grand Rapids: Zondervan Publishing House, 1975

Dake, Finis. *Dake's Annotated Reference Bible.* Lawrenceville: DBS, 1963/1991

Hagin, Kenneth E. *Man on Three Dimenions.* Tulsa: RHEMA Bible Church, 1973

Helps Word-Studies Lexicon. Retrieved from Biblehub.com. 1987, 2011

Houdmann, Michael S. *Got Questions? (miscellaneous).* Retrieved from https://www. gotquestions.org/, 2002-2025

Kirkwood, David. *Your Best Year Yet!* Pittsburgh: Ethnos Press, 1996

Lindsey, Hal. *The Liberation of Planet Earth.* New York: HarperCollins, 1974

LORD, The. *The Amplified Bible.* Grand Rapids: Zondervan, 1987

LORD, The. *Douay-Rheims Version. Holy Bible.* Gastonia: Tan books, 2009

LORD, The. *English Standard Version (ESV). Holy Bible.* Chicago: Crossway, 2001

LORD, The. *The International Standard Version New Testament.* Highlands Ranch: Davidson Press, 1998

LORD, The. *King James Version. Holy Bible.* Iowa Falls: World Bible Publishers

LORD, The. *New International Version (Revised). Holy Bible.* Nashville: Holman, 2011

LORD, The. *New King James Version Study Bible: Second Edition. Holy Bible.* Nashville: Thomas Nelson, 2012

LORD, The. *New Revised Standard Version. Holy Bible.* Nashville: Nelson, 1989

LORD, The. *Quest Study Bible: New International Version. Holy Bible.* Grand Rapids: Zondervan, 2003

LORD, The. *Young's Literal Translation Bible.* South Shore: Book Shed, 2016

Milne, Bruce. *Know the Truth.* Downers Grove: InterVarsity Press, 1982, 1998

MacArthur, John. *The MacArthur Study Bible.* Nashville: Word Bibles, 1997

Robertson, Pat. *ANSWERS to 200 of Life's Most Probing Questions.* Nashville: Thomas Nelson, 1984

Servant, David. *Heaven Word Daily.* Pittsburgh: Ethnos Press, 2009

Strong, James. *Strong's Exhaustive Concordance.* Grand Rapids: Baker, 1991

Vine, W.E. *Vine's Expository Dictionary of Biblical Words.* Cambridge: Nelson, 1985

Waren, Dirk. *Fountain of Life Teaching Ministry.* Retrieved from http://www.fountainoflifetm.com/, 2011-2025

Waren, Dirk. *HELL KNOW!* Youngstown: Soaring Eagle Press, 2014/2016

Waren, Dirk. *SHEOL KNOW!* Youngstown: Soaring Eagle Press, 2015/2024

Weymouth, Robertson. *New Testament in Modern Speech.* Pilgrim Press, 1932

Fountain of Life

Teaching Ministry

(Psalm 36:9)

The mission of Fountain of Life is to **set the captives FREE** by **reaching the world** with the **life-changing truths of God's Word**, the **power of the Holy Spirit** and the **Awesome News of the message of Jesus Christ**.

We're calling Spiritual Warriors all over the Earth to RISE UP and fulfill your calling!

Books by Dirk Waren:

The Believer's Guide to FORGIVENESS & WARFARE
Legalism Unmasked
HELL KNOW! (full and condensed versions)
SHEOL KNOW! (full and condensed versions)
The Four Stages of SPIRITUAL GROWTH
ANGELS: Their Purpose and Your Responsibility
THE LAW and the Believer
The SIX BASIC DOCTRINES of Christianity
GRACE: What Is It? How Do You Grow in It?
How to Handle OFFENSES: Personal & Criminal
WOMEN IN MINISTRY ...in God's Service
The FIVEFOLD MINISTRY Gifts: Apostle, Prophet, Evangelist, Pastor, Teacher
Solomon's SONG OF SONGS and Issues of Love & Sex
QUESTIONS & ANSWERS From the Bible
SPIRITUAL WARRIOR: The Manual
HUMAN NATURE: Spirit, Mind and Flesh

www.ingramcontent.com/pod-product-compliance
Lightning Source LLC
Chambersburg PA
CBHW071356130726
47996CB00002B/958